JB CURIE
Poynter, Margaret.
Marie Curie : genius
researcher of radioactivity

MARIE CURIE

GENIUS RESEARCHER OF RADIOACTIVITY

Margaret Poynter

Enslow Publishers, Inc.
40 Industrial Road
Box 398
Berkeley Heights, NJ 07922
USA

http://www.enslow.com

Originally published as *Marie Curie: Discoverer of Radium* in 2008.

Library of Congress Cataloging-in-Publication Data

Poynter, Margaret.
  Marie Curie : genius researcher of radioactivity / Margaret Poynter.
    pages cm. — (Genius scientists and their genius ideas)
  Originally published: 1994.
  Includes bibliographical references and index.
  Audience: Grades 4-6.
  ISBN 978-0-7660-6580-2
  1. Curie, Marie, 1867-1934—Juvenile literature. 2. Chemists—Poland—Biography—Juvenile literature. I. Title.
  QD22.C8P69 2015
  540.92—dc23
  [B]
                          2014031255

Future editions:
Paperback ISBN: 978-0-7660-6581-9
EPUB ISBN: 978-0-7660-6582-6
Single-User PDF ISBN: 978-0-7660-6583-3
Multi-User PDF ISBN: 978-0-7660-6584-0

Printed in the United States of America
102014 Bang Printing, Brainerd, Minn.
10 9 8 7 6 5 4 3 2 1

To Our Readers:
We have done our best to make sure all Internet Addresses in this book were active and appropriate when we went to press. However, the author and the publisher have no control over and assume no liability for the material available on those Internet sites or on other Web sites they may link to. Any comments or suggestions can be sent by e-mail to comments@enslow.com or to the address on the back cover.

☘ Enslow Publishers, Inc., is committed to printing our books on recycled paper. The paper in every book contains 10% to 30% post-consumer waste (PCW). The cover board on the outside of each book contains 100% PCW. Our goal is to do our part to help young people and the environment too!

CONTENTS

Chapter 1

Marie's Childhood Years

In December 1903, Marie Curie wrote a letter to her brother. "Dear Joseph," she said, "I thank you most tenderly for your letters. Don't forget to thank Manyusya [Joseph's daughter] for her little letter, so well written, which gave me great pleasure."

Marie said that she had been sick. Then she said that she and her husband, Pierre, had been honored with a Nobel Prize. "With much effort," she wrote, "we have avoided the banquets people wanted to organize in our honor."[1]

The Nobel Prize! What exciting news! Most winners would not have written about anything else. To Marie, though, there was only one good thing about the prize. The money would let Pierre quit one of his teaching jobs. He would get more rest.

The Price of Fame

Marie did not care about the prize itself. Now, hundreds of people wanted to talk to her and take her picture. Marie was very timid. She did not like talking to strangers and having people stare at her.[2] And these people were keeping her away from her work. To Marie, work was much more important than fame. She wanted to be left alone in her laboratory.

The "laboratory" was a leaky shed with a dirt floor. It was here that the Curies had discovered radium. The discovery changed science forever.

Roots

Marie Curie was born on November 7, 1867, in Warsaw, Poland. Her father, Vladislav Sklodowski, and her mother, Bronislawa, were teachers. She had three older sisters, Hela, Zosia and Bronya, and a brother, Joseph. They all called Marie by her nickname, Manya.

At this time, Poland was ruled by Russia. Russian was the official language and Russian books were used in the schools. The Russians forced Manya's father to take a low-paying job. To save money, the family moved into a smaller apartment and took in boarders. When Manya's mother became ill with tuberculosis,

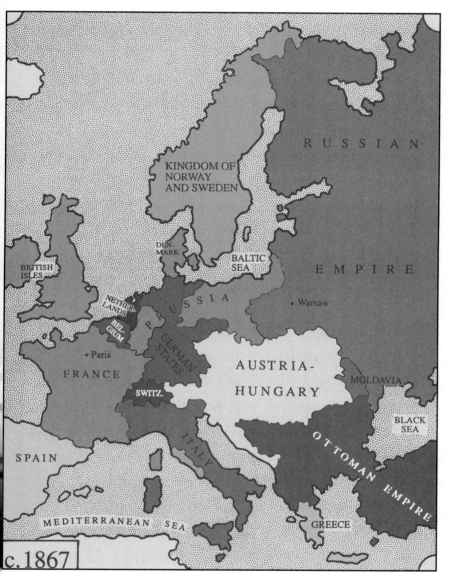

c.1867

When Marie was born, Poland was part of the Russian Empire.
Many modern European countries were a part of larger empires
at that time.

five-year-old Manya watched her become thin and pale. Every night, she prayed that her mother would get well.

Two years later, Zosia and Bronya became ill with typhus. They shook with chills and were covered with a rash. In spite of Manya's prayers, Zosia died. When Manya was ten, her mother also died. She decided that praying was a waste of time. She and her sisters put their faith in science. They pretended that they were doctors working to find a miracle cure.

Despite all their problems, Manya's father saw to it that his children were well educated. He taught them Polish history and the Polish language. He answered all their questions about science and nature. At school, though, Manya had a difficult time. The Russian teachers treated the Polish students unfairly. If they spoke even one word in Polish, they were punished.

Occasionally, a Russian inspector visited the classroom. The Polish students were afraid of him. If they gave the wrong answers to his questions, he said they were disloyal to Russia, and their parents were punished. One day, the inspector asked Manya some questions. She was so nervous that when he left, she burst into tears.[3]

But Manya was not discouraged. She eagerly studied history, language, mathematics, and literature. When she was just sixteen, she graduated as the top student in her class. She liked her gold medal, but she did not like shaking the hand of a Russian official or the Russian books she was given. Manya hated everything that came from that country.

Graduation

By the time she graduated, Marie was exhausted. Her father sent her to the country for a year so she could rest. When she returned, her father was ill and could no longer take in boarders. Marie had to find a job, but there were few jobs for well-educated Polish women. For a while she made a little money tutoring children. To give the lessons, she often walked across town in rain and in snow. If the students were lazy and failed their lessons, the parents blamed Manya. Many times, they refused to pay her.

Manya did not want to be a tutor forever. She dreamed of becoming a scientist, but the Russians did not allow women to go to college. Fortunately, she was able to attend the illegal "Floating University," in which 200 students met under cover of night in different houses. If the Russian police had found them, the students could have been sent to prison.

To Manya, the Floating University was a dream come true. Here, she read books in the Polish language and learned the true history of her country. She

Marie (Manya) had three sisters and a brother. From left to right are Bronya, Joseph, Marie, Hela, and Zosia.

performed experiments in physics and chemistry. She found that in other countries, students could ask questions without being punished. Manya wanted Poland to be such a country.[4] She taught other Polish women to read and write. People who are educated will not accept tyranny, she thought. They will help drive the Russians out of Poland.

A Broken Heart

Manya decided that she wanted to study science, and Bronya wanted to go to medical school. They decided to go to Paris, France, where women were allowed to go to a university. But their father could not afford to send both of them. Manya believed that she should get a job and help her older sister pay for her education. When Bronya graduated, she could work and pay Manya's expenses.

"Why should I be the first to go? . . . You are so gifted—probably more gifted than I am," Bronya said. "You should be the first to go."

"No!" Manya replied. And that was the end of the discussion.[1]

Leaving Home

When Bronya left for Paris, Manya took a job as a governess in Warsaw. A few months later, she found a job in a village 150 kilometers away. There, she could make more money, but she was unhappy as she boarded the train. She was leaving her family for the first time in her life.

The people Manya now worked for were wealthy, but most of the nearby families were poor. Many of the children did not go to school, and when they did, they were taught in Russian. Manya decided to teach the children their native language and their country's history. If she were caught, she might be put in prison, but she did not care.

Manya turned her room into a school, and was soon giving the children their first lesson. Her students were poorly dressed, and their hands and faces were dirty. They would not sit still, and they talked out of turn. But Manya patiently wrote the letters of the Polish alphabet on the blackboard. She formed the letters into words. The children began to listen and to copy the words into their notebooks. Day by day, they learned to read and write in their own language.

Manya was happy with their progress, but at the same time she was unhappy because she was not in school. In a letter to a friend, she wrote: "It will be five years before Bronya graduates and I can go to the university. What about Father? By that time, he will be old and might need me to take care of him. When can I return to school? Maybe never. My plans for the future? I have none."[2]

A Passion for Science

Most young girls would not have written such sad words. They would be going to parties and dances, but Manya preferred to spend her time reading about physics and chemistry. That Christmas, though, her employer's son, Casimir, came home for a visit. When he asked her to go on a picnic, she put her books aside. The next day, they went on a long walk. As the days passed, they fell in love, and when Casimir asked Manya to marry him, she said yes. Her happiness ended when Casimir's parents would not let him marry her. She is just a governess, they said. She is not good enough for you.

Now Manya felt hopeless. She had lost the man she loved. Her employers, whom she had thought of as her friends, considered her just a servant. Worst of all, she did not know if she would ever be able to go to school. She would have gone back to Warsaw, but she needed the job to help Bronya finish school.

Manya tried to write cheerful letters to her family and friends. But once she told Joseph that she had lost the hope of ever becoming anybody. To a friend, she wrote that she would give half her life to become independent, "if only I did not have to think of Bronya." Soon, though, Manya realized that her future was in her own hands. She turned back to her studies and wrote to the same friend, "First principle: Never to let one's self be beaten down by persons or events."[3]

Good News

By 1889, Manya had been a governess for four years, and suddenly there was good news. Her father had found a job that paid him a good salary. He could now send money to Bronya, so Manya left her job and returned to Warsaw. Here, she went to work for another wealthy family.

One year later, Bronya graduated and became engaged to another doctor. "In just a few more months," she told Manya, "you can come to Paris and live with me and my husband." And she could attend the Sorbonne, a famous university.

Oh, how Manya wanted to accept the invitation! But what about her father? Who would take care of him as he grew older? But it was her father who insisted that she go to Paris.

Monsieur Sklodowski with his daughters Marie, Bronya, and Hela.

During her last few months in Warsaw, Manya continued to tutor students, and she also attended the Museum of Industry and Agriculture. The "museum" was really a laboratory where Polish students could secretly study science. To Manya, the museum was a magical place. Here, she could spend hours doing the experiments she had read about. Sometimes, she was successful. Often, though, she would be in "the deepest despair because of accidents and failures."[4] But even when the results were bad, Manya was so excited that she had trouble sleeping. And when she did sleep, she dreamed about her work.

Finally, in the fall of 1891, at the age of twenty-four, Manya was ready to leave Warsaw. Soon she would be studying at the Sorbonne. She would be working in a modern laboratory. At last her dreams were coming true. Her real life was about to begin.

Chapter 3

FREEDOM

Despite her excitement, it was difficult for Manya to say goodbye to her father. She promised him that she would return in two or three years, and then she would never leave him again. Her father wished her luck and told her to work hard. After a three-day train trip, she arrived in Paris. She soon realized that she was now in a different world from the one she had known. Here, people spoke any language they wanted to speak. They were not afraid to say what they thought. The bookstores contained books from all over the world.

Here, there was true freedom, something that Manya had never experienced.

The Sorbonne

On November 3, Manya enrolled at the Sorbonne. She was one of only 23 women out of 1,825 students in the School of Science. To celebrate her new life, she wrote her real name, "Marie Sklodowska," on the admission papers. (In Polish, Sklodowska is the feminine form of Sklodowski.)

Marie had done well in her Polish classes of science and mathematics. She found, however, that the students who had gone to school in Paris had taken more advanced classes. Also, she did not speak and read French well, so she had to spend every spare hour studying. Actually, since she was very shy, she would rather study than meet new people. The few friends she did make were as serious about science as she was.

For a while, Marie lived with Bronya and her husband. To get back and forth to school, she spent two hours a day on a horse-drawn bus. Bronya's apartment was often filled with patients and with noisy visitors, so Marie decided to move close to school. She rented a tiny attic apartment that was hot in the summer and freezing cold during the winter. For heat, there was an old coal stove, but sometimes she could not afford coal. Then her fingers grew numb and ice formed in her water pitcher. The only light came from a small hole in the roof and a flickering oil lamp. Many times she had just bread and tea for dinner and fruit for lunch. But she was happy. Here it was quiet.

"I was entirely absorbed in the joy of learning and understanding," she later wrote. "All that I saw and learned that was new delighted me."[1]

One day, though, Marie fainted from hunger and lack of sleep. Bronya forced her to come back to her apartment, where she rested and ate steak, potatoes, and thick soup. After only one week, she thanked her sister and returned to her own apartment. To Marie, learning was more important than heat or food.

Top of the Class

Two years later, in July 1893, Marie had to take the final test for her master's degree. What if I fail? she asked herself. Will I have to return to Poland and work as a governess?[2] She was so nervous that it seemed as if the letters were dancing around on the page. Several minutes passed before she was able to answer the first question.[3]

Several days later she and the other students gathered to hear the test results. The professor began reading the names, starting with the highest score. And the first name he read was Marie Sklodowska!

Marie was the first woman to be awarded a physics degree at the Sorbonne. In 1894, at the age of twenty-six, she also obtained a master's degree in mathematics.

Marriage was not in her plans. All she wanted to do was finish her education, become a teacher, and be near her father. The two of them could work together to free Poland from the Russians.

A Change in Plans

Marie's plans changed when she met Pierre Curie, a French scientist. Marie liked his peaceful expression and his soft voice. He gave her helpful advice about the research she was doing. They took long walks and talked about their families and various scientific projects. Then Marie told him that she would not be going to school in the fall. She planned to return to Poland and get a job.

"Promise me that you will come back," Pierre said. "You have no right to abandon science."

Marie felt that what he was really saying was "You have no right to abandon me."

"I believe you are right," she replied. "I should like to come back—very much."[4]

On July 26, 1895, Marie and Pierre were married. It was a simple ceremony with no rings and no parties. Marie did buy a new suit for the wedding. It was black, so she could later wear it to the laboratory and not worry about stains. For a honeymoon, she and Pierre went on a bicycling trip.

Pierre and Marie greatly enjoyed bicycling in the country together.

Marie was now busier than ever. She had to learn to shop and to cook. She had to study and teach a class. And then her daughter, Irene, was born in 1897. She was grateful to Pierre's father, who offered to babysit. With his help she could pursue a doctor's degree.

For this degree she had to write a thesis, which is a report based on new and original research. Her first task was to find a subject for her research. Wilhelm Roentgen had recently discovered X-rays, which were able to pass through solid substances, such as wood and flesh. Pierre suggested that Marie study the work of Henri Becquerel, who was trying to find out where X-rays get their energy. He had left uranium salts in the sun and found that they produced rays that passed through black paper. It seemed to him that uranium must get its energy from sunlight. However, the uranium produced rays even when it had been kept in a dark drawer. Becquerel realized that the energy must come from the uranium itself.

Other scientists had shown little interest in Becquerel's work. But Marie started asking herself the same questions he was asking. Where does uranium get its energy? What is the nature of those rays? Is uranium the only element that emits such rays?[5]

Marie decided to find the answers to those questions. It was December 1897, and she had found the subject for her doctoral thesis.

An Exciting Discovery

Marie started her work in A small room that had been used for storage. Becquerel had found that uranium rays "ionize" air, or turn it into a conductor of electricity. Marie's first job was to measure the strength of uranium's electrical charge. She used an electrometer with a special detector that had been developed by Pierre and his brother, Jacques. This instrument gave very accurate electrical readings.

Marie tested pure uranium, uranium compounds, dry uranium, wet uranium, solid and powdered uranium and samples that had been exposed to darkness, light, heat, and cold. In every case, uranium ionized air by emitting rays that were steady and even. Their intensity was affected only by the amount of uranium that she used.

It was evident that the radiation had come from within the uranium itself. She called this feature "radioactivity." Was uranium the only element that was radioactive? Marie tested all the known chemical elements. She found that gold and copper were not radioactive, but others, thorium, for instance, were. Eventually, she tested pitchblende, a black, tarry ore. To her amazement, pitchblende was four times more radioactive than pure uranium.

The Mystery of Radiation

Where does this strong radiation come from? Marie wondered. Could this ore contain a second radioactive substance? Could that substance be an unknown element? Marie felt that it was, but to prove it, she would have to separate it from the pitchblende.

"The new element is there," she wrote to Bronya, "and I've got to find it."[1]

Pierre was so excited that he left his own work to help Marie. "Neither of us could see," she wrote later, "that in the beginning of this work, we were to enter the path of a new science which we should follow for all of our future."[2]

Pitchblende is composed of thirty different elements. To find the radioactive elements, Marie had to grind the ore into powder, then use various chemicals

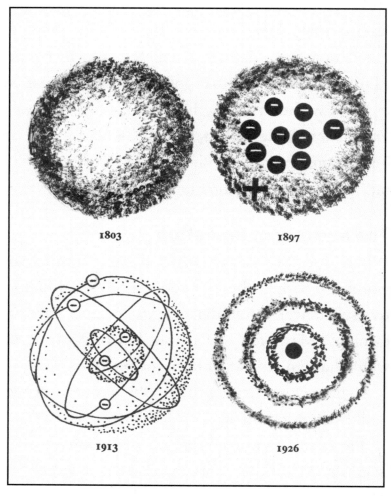

Scientists' concept of the atom changed greatly from the early nineteenth century to the twentieth century. In 1803, it was seen as a sphere-like fog of material. By 1926, the Bohr model—with the negative electrons circling the positively charged nucleus in various levels (or "shells")—was the definitive version.

to separate out, or isolate, each element. Pierre measured the radioactivity of these elements. One was 150 times more radioactive than uranium. A later one was 400 times more radioactive than uranium.

The New Elements

Marie was so certain that she had found a new element that she gave it a name—"polonium," after her homeland. She then isolated the polonium from the pitchblende. To her surprise, the remaining pitchblende was still radioactive. There must be *another* unknown element, she decided. And it was many times more radioactive than uranium! Marie named it "radium," from the Latin word for ray.

After they had announced their discovery, the Curies' real work began. Most scientists did not believe in "spontaneous radiation." They wanted to know the source of the radioactivity. To accept polonium and radium, they had to see them, touch them, examine them, and weigh them.

Radium's rays were much stronger than those of polonium, so Marie decided to focus on finding a pure sample of that element. She knew the search would be difficult. She and Pierre had estimated that uranium formed only one percent of pitchblende. They later found that it formed only one millionth of one

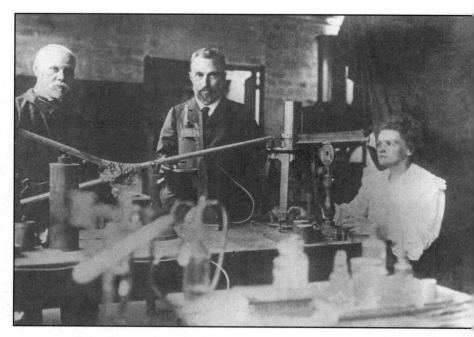

Pierre and Marie Curie at work in the laboratory circa 1900

percent. Just to begin their work, they would need a lot of the ore. Fortunately, the manager of an Austrian uranium-producing plant gave them a ton of it. To him it was worthless, because he had already removed most of the uranium. He was glad to give it to the "two French lunatics who thought they needed it."[3]

The Curies needed more room for their research, so they moved into a drafty shed with a leaky roof, peeling walls, and a dirt floor. It contained only an old stove, a table, and a blackboard. A friend called it a cross between a stable and a potato cellar, but Marie did not care about the way it looked.

The ore was delivered in April 1898. Marie immediately started the painstaking process of isolating the elements. Day after day, week after week, she sorted, ground, dissolved, and filtered small batches of pitchblende. Standing over a large cauldron, she stirred boiling, poisonous mixtures with an iron rod almost as tall as she was. The fumes stung her nose and throat. By nightfall she ached with fatigue. In the winter she grew numb from the cold. During the summer she suffered from the heat.

Pierre measured each element's electrical charge. He had to fight to keep out drops of water from the leaky roof and the dust that rose from the floor. But the samples he was able to save showed more and more radioactivity.

Four years passed, during which the Curies treated eight tons of pitchblende. Finally, by March 1902 they had extracted one-tenth of one gram of the precious substance. It was 900 times more radioactive than uranium. In the darkness of night, it glowed silvery-white, and the vials were outlined in blue. To Marie they looked like glow worms or faint fairy lights.

Pierre had once said that he hoped radium would have a beautiful color. His hope had become a reality.

Chapter 5

PROBLEMS

In 1903 Marie received her doctor's degree. She had a strong marriage and a healthy daughter. Her work with radium was going well. She should have been completely happy, but there were some big problems.

One was that she and Pierre had barely enough money for food and rent. To pay their bills they had to teach classes. Both of them disliked having to spend so much time away from their research.

Another was that Marie's father had died, and she had not been able to see him during his final days. She comforted herself with the knowledge that he knew she had found her radium.[1] When one of Bronya's children died, Marie shared her grief and started worrying that Irene might get sick.

Her own health and that of Pierre were an ongoing problem. They were always tired. Marie had lost some twenty pounds and coughed so much that she became weak and breathless. Pierre's legs were so painful that he could not sleep and had trouble walking.

When Pierre said, "It's pretty hard, this life we have chosen," Marie was frightened. She had never heard him complain. Was his health worse than she had imagined? What if he died? "We cannot exist without each other, can we?" she said.

"You are wrong," Pierre replied. "Whatever happens, if one has to go on like a body without a soul, one must work just the same."[2]

Continuing Research

Marie knew he was right. With renewed energy, the Curies threw themselves back into their research. They found that radium is two million times more radioactive than uranium. Its rays pass easily through lighter materials. They give off so much heat that radium melts its own weight in ice within an hour. If it is wrapped in paper, it reduces the paper to powder.

Their tests showed that anything the radium rays touched became radioactive. The dust in the shed, the air they breathed, and the food they ate as they worked

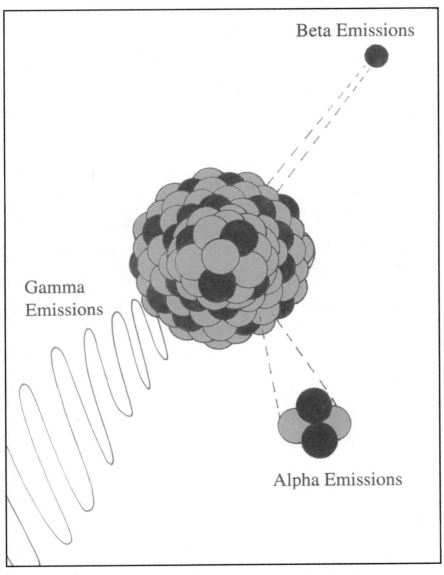

Atoms give off three types of radioactive particles: alpha emissions (neutrons), beta emissions (electrons and positrons), and gamma emissions.

were all radioactive. The Curies' hands were scarred from old burns and blistered from new ones.

Pierre became curious about how radium affects various living tissues. He folded some radium salts into a bandage and taped it to his arm. The skin quickly reddened, and an open sore appeared. Although he removed the bandage after only a few hours, the sore took months to heal.

If radium destroys healthy tissue, what will it do to diseased tissue? Pierre wondered. He applied radium to the cancerous tumors in some animals. The cancer cells were destroyed. Pierre's mother had died from cancer. He realized that with this treatment, perhaps she could have survived. Someday, he thought, radium will save countless lives. He showed a vial of the glowing substance to some friends and said, "Here is the light of the future!"[3]

World Reaction

Scientists all over the world were reading about radium and begging for a sample of the element. Radium was worth more than gold. The Curies could have sold their samples, then patented the extraction method and charged for its use. They could have become millionaires, but they did not think that radium

This famous caricature of the Curies, "Radium," first ran in the popular British periodical Vanity Fair *on December 22, 1904.*

belonged to them. It belonged to the people who needed it. To make money from it would have been contrary to the scientific spirit.

Still, they could not help thinking about what they could have done with all that money. They were once invited to a banquet in London. Pierre wore his worn, everyday coat. Marie wore a plain black dress with no jewelry. All the other women in the room wore expensive silk gowns and diamond necklaces and emerald rings. Marie and Pierre amused themselves by calculating how many fine laboratories could have been built with all those "doo-dads."[4]

In November 1903 the Curies received a telegram from Sweden. Along with Antoine Becquerel, they had won the Nobel Prize in physics for their work with radium. Soon, the names of Pierre and Marie would be known the world over. And their lives would be changed forever.

Chapter 6

A Tragedy

The Nobel Prizes are given out in Stockholm, Sweden. A French official accepted the Curies' award for them, because they were too busy to take the trip. Besides, neither of them felt well enough to give speeches and meet strangers. They just wanted to be with their family and do their work.

But no one seemed to care what they wanted. The couple received hundreds of letters and telegrams. They were invited to speak at meetings, and banquets were given in their honor. Newspaper and magazine reporters followed them from their home to the shed and back again. If Marie went to the market, people crowded around her. They wanted to talk with her, to touch her. They wanted to see Irene. They even wanted to see the family cat. The Curies were seldom alone at home or at work.

Marie had always been timid, and all the attention frightened her. "Our life has been altogether spoiled by honors and fame," she wrote to Joseph.[1] In a later letter she wrote that "one would like to dig into the ground somewhere to find a little peace."[2] To find that little peace she and Pierre went to the beach for a few days. Even here a reporter found Marie sitting on the front steps of a fisherman's cottage. He asked her about her work and how she felt about winning a Nobel Prize. She answered his questions until he asked about her family and her childhood.

"In science," she replied, "we must be interested in things, not in persons."[3] She then rose to go into the cottage. The interview was over.

One good thing came with the Nobel Prize. The Curies received a large amount of money. Marie shared it with her family and several people who had helped her. She also gave money to poor Polish students and replaced the scholarship money she had received at the Sorbonne.

Pierre quit one of his jobs and hired a laboratory assistant.

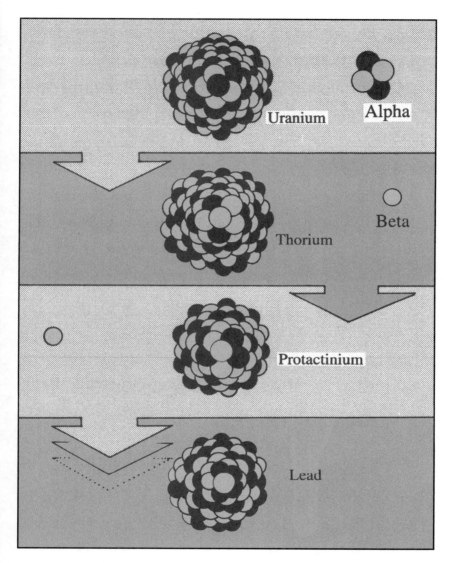

Radioactive (or unstable) elements break down into different elements during radioactive decay. Here, uranium goes through several stages before finally becoming lead (a stable element).

Failing Health

Marie hoped that Pierre's health would improve with more rest. While they were in London he was so weak that he needed help getting dressed. During the lecture his fingers were so sore that he spilled some of the radium sample. Every day he suffered from vicious attacks of pain.

Marie was worried about his illness, but she herself was always tired. She wished people would leave her alone. She almost wished she had never heard of radium. She was not even cheered up when she found she was expecting another child. Life is too hard, she thought, even for children.

Marie's second daughter, Eve, was born in December 1904. The birth left her feeling more tired than ever, and she did nothing but sleep. As weeks passed, though, she began to feel better. A visit from Bronya helped, as did the smiles of her newborn child. She felt well enough to teach classes again and looked forward to continuing her research. The Sorbonne had given the Curies space in a laboratory on the school grounds.

Both Marie and Pierre had dreamed of working in a fine laboratory. Still, Marie was overcome by sadness when they closed the door of the shed for the last time. "It was in that miserable old shed that we passed the best and happiest years of our lives," she later wrote.

On Easter Sunday in 1906, the Curies took their children to the country. The next day they watched Irene and Eve romp on the grass. Pierre turned to Marie and touched her hair. "Life has been sweet with you," he murmured.[4] That afternoon the family picked flowers. Later, Pierre went back to Paris. Marie and the children followed on Wednesday. The weather was cold, a sharp wind was blowing, and rain beat upon the windows.

A Terrible Loss

On Thursday, April 19, it was still raining. The skies were dark. That morning Marie was busy with the children when Pierre called good-bye and left to go to a meeting.

Marie had several errands to do that day. She told Pierre's father that she would be back around noon. But she was delayed and did not return until six o'clock. Two of Pierre's friends were waiting for her. Marie looked at them. She looked at Pierre's father.

"Pierre was run over by a cart," one of the friends said. "He is dead." He went on to describe the accident. Pierre had not been paying attention when he crossed the street. The driver of the heavy, horse-drawn wagon had yelled a warning, but it was too late. The rear wheels ran over Pierre.

There was a long silence. Marie did not move or cry out. Finally, in a low voice, she murmured, "Pierre is dead? Dead? Absolutely dead?"[5]

"Yes," Pierre's father replied. He held out his arms to Marie.

Marie looked at the flowers they had picked in the country. They were still fresh. In a daze, she walked into the garden. The trees were wet from the rain. They dripped water on her, but she did not notice. She sat on a wet bench, bowed her head, and covered her face with her hands.[6]

As the days passed, Pierre's death seemed to have taken the life out of Marie. Family and friends tried to comfort her, but she did not listen when they spoke. She stared blankly into space and seemed not to take notice of anyone or anything.

Meanwhile, there were questions that had to be answered quickly. Who would continue Pierre's research at the Sorbonne? Who would take charge of the laboratory? Who would teach his classes? Marie did not seem to care. But Bronya and Jacques, Pierre's brother, talked to the school officials. They said that Marie should carry on Pierre's work and teach his classes. She should be put in charge of the laboratory.

"But no woman has ever been given such work!" the officials exclaimed. Bronya and Jacques said that there was no one else who would be able to do it. In the end the officials had no choice but to agree.

Marie had been offered a pension by the French government, but she refused it. "I am young enough to earn my living and that of my children," she said.[7] But she was hesitant about taking over Pierre's jobs, even when Pierre's father said she should.

Her decision was made when she recalled Pierre's words: "Whatever happens . . . one must work."

On a Monday morning the following November, Marie entered a crowded lecture hall at the Sorbonne. Her face was pale. She was trembling. She stared straight ahead.

Suddenly there was a storm of applause. Marie straightened her shoulders and nodded. When the class quieted down, she began to speak.

"When one considers the progress that has been made in physics in the past ten years, one is surprised at the advance that has taken place in our ideas concerning electricity and matter."

The students were astounded. Professor Pierre Curie had ended his last lecture with that sentence. Professor Marie Curie was starting right where he had left off.

Chapter 7

LIFE WITHOUT PIERRE

Marie had to leave early every morning to teach at the Sorbonne. It was late in the afternoon when she returned home to spend time with Eve and Irene. But keeping busy did not help her recover from Pierre's death. It might have helped if she had shared her grief with others, but she would not let anyone comfort her or see her cry. In a diary she poured out her feelings to Pierre. "I want to tell you that I no longer love the sun or the flowers. . . . Everything is over. . . . I tried to take a measurement, but I felt the impossibility of going on."[1]

Even her children failed to help her get over her sorrow. Still, she took her daughters on long bicycling trips and went swimming with them and worked in the garden. She taught science and arithmetic to them and their friends. "You must get so you never make a mistake," she told them. "The secret is in not going too fast. And one must never dirty a laboratory table during an experiment."[2]

Carrying On

Marie believed that the simplest way was often the best way. As an example, she held up a jar of hot liquid and asked the youngsters to tell her the best way to keep it hot. The class discussed various methods. Marie simply smiled and put a lid on the jar.

But the time she spent with her children failed to bring her any real joy. Not even her research lifted her spirits. Then another scientist challenged Marie, saying that she had not measured radium's atomic weight beyond question. He said that its radioactivity alone did not ensure that it is an element. His ideas threatened the results of the Curies' years of toil.

Marie knew that Pierre would expect her to rise to the challenge. She started putting her research on a firmer basis. After months of painstaking work, she was finally able to obtain the exact measurements she needed. Now there was no doubt. Radium was added to the periodic table of elements.

After Pierre's death, Marie had to raise Eve and Irene by herself.

Pierre had always dreamed of having a first-class laboratory. Now Marie vowed to fulfill that dream and build a laboratory that was worthy of his memory. In 1907 Andrew Carnegie, a wealthy American, donated money for the project. Various French agencies also donated money for the Paris Radium Institute. Marie said that she wanted it to have large windows and a beautiful garden.

Several months later she was planting rose bushes in that garden. As she patted down the earth she felt at peace for the first time since Pierre's death. When she heard that the shed was going to be destroyed, she rushed to see it for the last time. Pierre's handwriting was still on the blackboard. For a moment she felt that the door might open and he would enter the room. Their research could continue. Their life together could go on.

She shook her head, then turned and left the shed. She did, after all, have work to do.

Another Prize

By 1910, when Pierre's father died, Marie had still not fully recovered from Pierre's death. She could not even bring herself to say "my husband" or "your father." Despite her ongoing sorrow, she wrote two books and acted as one of the directors of the Radium Institute. In 1911 she won the Nobel Prize in chemistry. No one else had ever won two Nobel Prizes.

Marie found that being famous and winning awards did not cause everyone to admire her. Some French people called her "that foreign woman." "She does not deserve to be honored," they said. "A woman should not be doing a man's work. Why doesn't she go to church? Why doesn't she want to talk to reporters? Why does she hide from people? She must be a bad person."

Some of her critics wondered why she had so many men friends. If they had asked Marie, she would have told them that most of her friends were scientists. And most scientists were men.

The gossip made Marie hate fame more than ever. In addition to that problem, her health was growing worse. Joseph, Hela, Jacques, and Bronya came to Paris to be with her. They persuaded her to enter a nursing home. There she rested and regained some of her strength, but then she had a kidney operation, during which she almost died. After spending almost all of 1912 relaxing in a friend's home, she was still so weak she could barely stand up.

Changes in Poland

One piece of good news raised her spirits. Russia was losing its hold on Poland. Its people were regaining their freedom, and some Polish scientists were planning to build a radioactivity laboratory in Warsaw. They asked Marie to be its director.

To Marie, Paris had become an unfriendly place, and she was tempted to take the offer. But she felt that Pierre would have wanted her to stay in Paris. Early in 1913 she went to Warsaw for the opening of the new laboratory. Polish citizens packed the hall. For the first time she gave a lecture in her native language. Everywhere she went her fellow Poles followed her, and she felt freedom in the air.

Hiking with Einstein

That summer Marie felt strong enough to hike through the Alps with her daughters. The group included a famous scientist, Albert Einstein. He and Marie exchanged ideas and talked about their research. One day Einstein was quiet as the hikers were climbing up a steep rock along a deep crevasse. He seemed to be deep in thought, and Marie was afraid that he was not watching his footing. She braced herself when he suddenly stopped and grabbed her arm.

"You understand," he said, "what I need to know is exactly what happens to the passengers in an elevator when it falls into emptiness."[3]

While everyone else in the group laughed at his remark, Marie was silent. To her it did not sound silly or out of place. She understood that he was thinking about gravity. As with Marie, Einstein's work was always on his mind.

Chapter 8

A WORLD AT WAR

In July 1914 Marie's laboratory in the Paris Radium Institute was finished. Carved above the door were these words: *Institute du Radium, Pavillon Curie* (Institute of Radium, Curie Pavilion).

These buildings "are the temples of the future," Marie said. "It is here that humanity grows bigger, strengthens and betters itself."[1]

She was eager to start her job as director, but first she wanted to take a vacation. Irene and Eve and their governess had already gone to a beach cottage. Marie planned to join them on August 3, but by that time, war had broken out in Europe. On August 2 the German army invaded France. There would be no vacation.

Three German bombs fell on the city of Paris on September 2. By now only Marie and a mechanic with heart trouble remained at the institute. All the other men on the staff had been drafted into the military service. Marie's research would have to wait for peacetime. Meanwhile, she felt there must be something she could do to help France in its war effort.

Aiding the War Effort

"I am resolved to put all my strength at the service of my adopted country," she wrote in a letter to a friend.[2] She was worried about her family in Poland, but there was nothing she could do to help them or her native land. When the French government asked for gold and silver, she offered to donate all of her medals, including the two Nobel medals.

As the German troops approached Paris, the government was moved to Bordeaux. It was decided that the radium was too valuable to be left behind. Marie packed it in a lead box and boarded the train, which was jammed with people and baggage. None of the passengers knew that what she was carrying was worth a million francs. After the radium was stored in a safe-deposit box in Bordeaux, Marie took the next train back to Paris.

During World War I, Marie Curie aided the war effort by turning cars into mobile X-ray units.

There was no time to rest. Doctors needed X-ray equipment to locate broken bones and bullets inside soldiers' bodies. Marie collected the equipment from the Sorbonne, her laboratory, and from the companies that made the machines. She then convinced French officials to let her set up radiology centers. She pleaded with military officers to give her supplies. At first some of them refused. They did not want to be bothered by civilians. But Marie was stubborn. Her nagging always got her what she wanted.

Marie knew that the soldiers on the front lines and in base hospitals were in desperate need of X-rays. She talked wealthy people into donating their cars, then had the cars transformed into mobile X-ray units. Within a short time twenty of these "petite Curies" (little Curies) were ready to follow the troops from place to place. Marie herself learned how to drive one of them, change its tires, and clean its dirty carburetor. She was often seen turning a crank to start a balky engine.

After taking an anatomy course and one in the use of X-ray equipment, Marie started training people to staff the other mobile units and the 200 permanent X-ray units that were being set up. Seventeen-year-old Irene became her first radiological assistant. Between the two of them, from 1916 to 1918, they trained 150 more assistants. Marie herself made hundreds of trips to the front lines.

Occasionally patrols stopped her from going closer to the battlefield. "What's a woman doing out here?" some of them asked. After Marie showed them her official papers, they waved her on.[3]

A base hospital was often nothing but a bombed-out building, and there might be a hundred wounded soldiers waiting. Marie spent days in the darkroom developing X-rays. She ate when she had a minute. She slept wherever she could find a space. She did not mind the work or the discomfort. But it was difficult for both her and Irene to hide their emotions when they saw so many badly injured men. The satisfaction they received from helping the soldiers made up for any discomfort they felt.

"This was indeed a splendid reward for our years of toil," Marie said.

During the war Marie visited over 300 French and Belgian hospitals. Only a few people she met knew who she was. In Belgium, when she was mistaken for a nurse's helper, she smiled. She did not say that she knew the king and queen of their country.

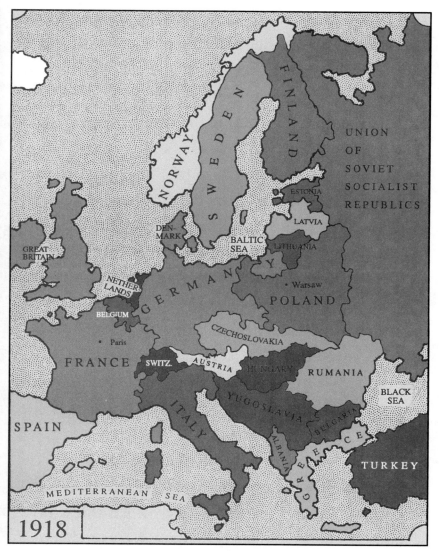

1918

After World War I, many of Europe's boundaries changed. Poland became an independent nation.

Returning to Paris

By 1915 all the X-ray units were staffed, so Marie started moving into her new laboratory. By that time it was unlikely that the Germans would overrun Paris, so she brought her gram of radium back to the city. Using an electric pump, she started collecting radon, a gas that is given off by radium. After sealing the radon in glass tubes, she sent it to hospitals. There, it was used to destroy diseased tissues and bad scars and sores.

Marie also set up radiology courses at the institute. Many of her students were young, poorly educated women who worked at low-paying jobs. After taking the courses, they were able to become aides to physicians or to work independently.

On November 11, 1918, Marie was working in her laboratory when she was startled by the sound of gunfire. She ran into the hall. "What is happening?" she asked an assistant.

"The war is over!" was the reply.

Trembling with joy, she rushed outside to join the cheering men and women who crowded the streets. France was now out of danger. Marie was even happier at the thought that her beloved Poland was free at last. Her lifelong dream had come true. She thought of all the students who had studied in secret in the Floating University. She thought of all the poor Polish women she had taught to read and write in their own language. They and thousands of others had made this day possible.

In her next letter to Joseph, Marie wrote, "We did not hope to live to see this moment ourselves. We thought it might not even be given to our children to see it, and it is here!"[4]

Marie had faced hardships and danger during the war. She would never forget the shrieks and moans of hundreds of wounded soldiers. Now, she herself was tired and ill. She had only a little money because she had given so much to aid in the war effort. Nevertheless, she was planning for her future. She wanted to return to the work she loved.

Chapter 9

A Trip to the United States

Instead of starting her research right away, Marie spent several weeks with Irene and Eve. They skated, hiked, and went horseback riding. She and Irene worked together in the laboratory. She rejoiced over Eve's progress in her career as a concert pianist. Slowly she started fully accepting Pierre's death.

Her health had seemed to improve, but she was annoyed by a constant, loud ringing in her ears. Since her eyesight was failing, she had trouble going up and down stairs and sometimes needed help crossing a street. She told no one about these problems. Her eye doctor knew her only as "Madame Carre."

Marie had long suspected that exposure to radium was the cause of her medical problems and those of Pierre. Neither of them had been protected from its rays. One of her friends, a scientist, had spilled some radioactive material on herself. A short time later she was dead. Another scientist had a tube of polonium explode in her face. Her hair fell out, and she had severe stomach problems. Others who worked with radium had sharp leg pains. Pierre Curie had suffered terribly from just such pains.

Marie set up rules to protect the people who worked in her laboratory. They had to use lead screens to intercept the rays. They were told to change their laboratory coats often. They were not allowed to touch the tubes of radium with their bare hands and were given regular blood tests.

Marie herself often did not follow her own rules. After all, she declared, she had worked with radium for many years and was still getting around very well.

Searching for Support

During the course of the war Marie had pleaded for help to set up her radiological services. Now she started pleading for supplies for the radium institute. Despite her shyness and stage fright, she talked to gatherings of wealthy people. One journalist said of Marie that "this great woman . . . was speaking haltingly, tremblingly. . . . She, who daily handles a particle of radium more dangerous than lightning, was afraid when confronted with the necessity of appearing before the public."[1]

Marie still disliked giving interviews. In May 1920, when an American magazine editor, Marie "Missy" Meloney, asked to see her, Marie said no. But Missy was as stubborn as Marie. She asked again and again, and finally Marie said yes.

During the interview Marie said that the research and therapy centers in the United States altogether had about fifty grams of radium, but the Paris institute still had only one gram, despite the fact that it was Marie who had discovered the element.

Missy was shocked. "If you had the whole world to choose from, what would you take?" she asked.

"I would choose another gram of radium to continue my research," Marie replied. "But I cannot afford it."[2]

When Missy returned to the United States, she formed the "Marie Curie Radium Campaign." The members of the committee wrote letters and made telephone calls to scientists and wealthy people. In less than a year they collected $100,000, which was enough to buy the radium.

"The money has been found," Missy wrote to Marie. "The radium is yours."

Coming to America

But Missy had one request. Many of the people who had donated money wanted to meet Marie. She had to go to the United States to get the radium. The thought of such a trip terrified Marie, but Missy would not take no for an answer. Irene and Eve also insisted that Marie make the trip, and they bought her four new dresses. Marie said that they had wasted their money, but four weeks later, she and her daughters boarded the S.S. *Olympic.* One of the first things Marie noticed was that when she opened the closet door in the cabin, the light went on. She went inside the closet and shut the door. The light went off. In and out, off and on, Marie tried to find the switch. Dinnertime arrived, and she was still trying to figure out how the light worked.

At New York harbor a huge crowd greeted the ship. There were troops of Girl Scouts. Hundreds of Polish immigrants waved red and white roses. American, French, and Polish flags waved in the breeze. Cameras clicked and flash bulbs went off.

"Look this way, Madame Curie," voices shouted. "Turn your head to the left! Lift your head! Look this way! This way! This way!"[3]

The scene was worse than Marie had ever imagined.

Marie Curie and President Harding (foreground) during Curie's visit to the White House in May 1921

During the next few weeks, Marie attended dinners in her honor. She made her way through crowds of people. Tearful men and women tried to kiss her hand. Female students waved flags and flowers. Hundreds of them surrounded her car, and she was afraid she would be crushed. She was even recognized when she visited the Grand Canyon. By this time her right arm was in a sling. An enthusiastic handshake had sprained her wrist.

On May 20, 1921, wearing the same black dress she had worn to the second Nobel ceremony, Marie went to the White House in Washington D.C. President Warren G. Harding called her a "noble creature." He spoke of her years of "crushing toil." He then passed a silken cord over her head. On that cord was the key to her container of radium.

The trip to the United States taught Marie an important lesson. As a student she had hidden in an attic. As a researcher she had hidden in her laboratory. But she was now a famous woman, and she could no longer hide. The fame that she had tried to avoid had brought her a gram of radium. Perhaps her fame could help bring other things that she wanted: world peace, the sharing of scientific knowledge, scholarships for poor college students. High on her list was a Warsaw radium institute where cancer patients could be treated.

Marie knew there was only way to reach her goals. She had to meet people. She had to talk to them and answer their questions. She had once said, "In science, we must be interested in things, not in persons."[4] She now knew better. Someone had to tell people about those "things," and she was going to have to be that someone.

Chapter 10

An Ordinary Day

The trip to the United States was just a beginning. Suddenly Marie was a world traveler. She went to Brazil, Spain, Italy, the Netherlands, England, and Switzerland. She visited laboratories and universities. She met kings and queens and presidents and asked each of them for more money for scientific research. Almost everyone found it hard to say no to this frail woman dressed in black. One observer said that she had the "moral force of a Buddhist monk."[1]

Marie went to Poland four times. She wanted to see her family, but she also wanted to raise money for a Warsaw radium clinic. With Bronya's help she flooded the country with posters. "Buy a brick for the Marie Sklodowska Institute," the posters read. Brick by brick, the walls started to go up.

Irene and Frederic

In 1926 Irene Curie married Frederic Joliot, who worked in the Paris Radium Institute. Now Marie had two helpers instead of just one. The three of them shared their worries and discussed their research and ideas. Eve, meanwhile, was becoming a well-known concert pianist.

When the Warsaw Radium Institute was completed, Bronya became its director. But the institute could not treat patients because it had no radium. Marie wrote to Missy, who immediately started another successful fund-raising drive. Again Missy's only request was that Marie come to the United States to receive the radium.

A Return to the U.S.

In 1929 Marie greeted the crowds as she had on the first trip, wearing a plain, black dress and carrying the same old brown handbag. Henry Ford gave her a car, and President Herbert Hoover invited her to stay overnight at the White House. Usually only important foreign officials stay overnight at the White House.

During her travels, one thing bothered Marie. "When they talk to me about my 'splendid work,'" she said, "it seems to me that I am already dead. . . . It seems to me that the services I might still render don't mean much to them."[2]

Marie Curie continued her lab work through most of her later life.

Words of praise meant nothing to Marie, nor did all the honors she received. As soon as she arrived home she put her medals and ribbons away. But she did keep out some of the banquet menus she had collected. They were made of heavy cardboard, and their backs had been perfect for many of her scribbled notes.

Marie's travels were an important way for her to raise money, but she was always glad to return to her work at the institute. Her own research now had to take second place to directing the laboratory. All day long reporters, students, and other scientists wanted to talk to her. Each day she received dozens of letters, many from cancer patients thanking her for discovering radium. Some were addressed to "Mme. Curie, Paris," or "Mme. Curie, scientist, Paris, France." The letters were always delivered.

The laboratory was often short of supplies. Marie went to various officials, sometimes pleading, sometimes demanding. Few of those officials dared to turn her down. One way or the other she always got what she wanted.

After twenty-five years of teaching classes Marie still had a fear of public speaking. Nevertheless, she never missed her twice-a-week lectures to her students.

Her Greatest Pleasure

Marie Curie's greatest pleasure was working with her student researchers, who were organized into small teams to work on radioactivity projects. She consulted with each team every day, answering questions, giving advice, encouraging them, praising them, and scolding them when necessary.

These young men and women were like her family. When she was with them she could laugh and forget Pierre's absence and ignore her own worsening health problems. She was heartbroken when one of her favorite pupils drowned in a river.

"I am quite overcome," she wrote. "His mother said he had passed the best years of his life in the laboratory. What was the good of it, if it had to end like this?"[3]

When she found some spare time, Marie worked on her own research. Sometimes it did not go well. At those times she slumped into a chair and gazed into space. A student once asked her what was wrong.

"That polonium has a grudge against me," she muttered.[4]

Marie seldom arrived home before eight or nine o'clock. As she and Eve ate dinner, they often talked about how they could help the poor people of France. After dinner Marie went into her study, where she wrote science books and articles. She also worked on her autobiography, which Missy had asked her to write. At first Marie had objected.

"My life is such a simple little story," she said. "I was born in Warsaw of a family of teachers. I married Pierre Curie and have two children. I have done my work in France."

Marie seldom used her desk. She liked to sit on the floor, with her books and papers spread out around her, talking to herself in Polish. At two or three o'clock, she finally stood up and stretched.

"Ah, how tired I am," she said. And then she went to bed.

THE END

E ve and Irene did their best to get Marie to slow down. "You have worked hard all your life," they said. "Now you should rest."

But Marie refused to slow down. She continued to teach classes. She was overseeing the building of a factory for the processing of ores. She was writing Pierre's biography, along with other books. And she could not stop her research. Her laboratory was her life. The buzzing in her ears, her illnesses, her constant fever, her poor eyesight—nothing could keep her from her work.

To prove to others that she was healthy, Marie went skating, skiing, bicycling, and took long walks. In the spring of 1934 Bronya came to visit. Over the Easter holiday she and Marie went on a trip.

The weather was cold, and the house they had rented was poorly heated. Although Bronya held her close, Marie could not stop shivering. "Will I be able to finish my book?" she asked.

As the weather warmed up, Marie felt better. After a few more days of rest, she and Bronya returned to Paris. Bronya was still worried about her sister, but it was time for her to go back to Warsaw.

"Please see a doctor," she begged Marie.

"No, no. I'm all right," Marie replied. She hugged Bronya and said goodbye.

Marie continued to have good days and bad days. On the bad days, she stayed home and worked on her book. She was tired and weak even on the good days, but she managed to go to the laboratory. When she had chills and fever and a doctor told her to stay in bed, she insisted on going to work.

Later that day, her fever was so high that she had to go home. "Wait for me a little while," she told a group of students. "I am going to rest for a few days."[1]

On her way to her car she walked through the garden. She told the gardener to take care of a sickly looking rose bush.

As soon as she arrived home she went to bed and allowed Eve to call a doctor. He said that her lungs were inflamed and that she needed to go to a hospital in the mountains. There she could breathe clean air. Eve did not think that Marie was strong enough for the trip, but four more doctors agreed with the first.

Final Days

As they prepared for the trip, Marie talked to Eve about her research, about the Warsaw Radium Institute, and about Eve's future as a pianist. She said that she hoped Irene would win a Nobel Prize. (Irene and her husband, Frederic Joliot, did win the Nobel Prize for chemistry in 1935.)

Just before she left, Marie called her laboratory assistant. "I count on you to put everything in order," she said. "We shall resume this work after my holiday."[2]

The effort of talking caused Marie to grow still weaker. As she began her trip she ached all over and had a high fever. As soon as she arrived at the hospital she fainted. Eve knew that her mother might be dying, but she told the doctors she did not want her to be given any painful treatments.

"My mother is very sick," she wrote to Missy. "She is suffering so much I cannot bear to look at her. I have to go out of the room to cry."

For several days, Marie barely spoke, and then her mind began to wander. "I cannot express myself

Marie Curie near the end of her life. She died a short time after this picture was taken.

properly," she muttered. "My head is turning." "Was it made with radium or mesotherium?" "I am trembling so."

"I don't want it. I want to be left alone." she said as she refused a shot.[3]

Those were her last words. As dawn broke on July 4, 1934, Marie Curie's heart stopped beating. She was sixty-six years old, and her scarred hands were finally still.

The news of Marie's death quickly spread around the world. Bronya, Hela, and Joseph rushed to Paris. Marie's many friends were stunned by the news. Her students sobbed.

"We have lost everything," one of them wrote.

Marie was buried above Pierre. Irene and Joseph threw a handful of Polish soil into her grave. One year later her last book was published. *Radioactivity* was Marie Curie's last message to her young "lovers of physics."

ACTIVITIES

The Building Blocks of Science

In 1895, Wilhelm Roentgen discovered X-rays. These rays go through wood, cloth, and flesh. They do not go through thick lead and bone.

A few months later, Antoine Becquerel found that uranium gives off rays. These rays go through paper and glass. Because of this discovery, Becquerel shared the 1903 Nobel Prize in physics with Marie and Pierre Curie.

Marie Curie read and studied the work of Roentgen and Becquerel. What she learned helped her in her own work. Marie's discoveries, in turn, helped other scientists. Building block upon building block, scientific knowledge grows. Marie Curie's work helped form our modern world. We now have atomic power. We have atomic submarines. We have radiation treatments for cancer. Radioactive dating reveals the ages of rocks and fossils. Radiation finds cracks in machinery and in airplane parts. It measures the thickness of metal pipes. It preserves and sterilizes food.

Understanding radioactivity helps us understand how our sun works. Understanding our sun helps us understand our solar system. It helps us understand our whole universe.

Marie Curie died in 1934. But the legacy of her work will keep her memory alive forever.

Making a Thermometer

Marie Curie showed her students how to make a thermometer. Now you can make one, too. See how substances expand, or grow larger, when they are heated. See how substances contract, or grow smaller, when they are cooled.

Materials:

- a small soda bottle
- modeling clay
- a clear plastic drinking straw
- food coloring
- an index card

Procedure:

1. Fill the bottle about four-fifths full of water. Add some food coloring.

2. Dry the lip of the bottle. Squeeze some clay around the rim. Put the straw halfway into the bottle. Press the clay around the straw. Make a tight seal.

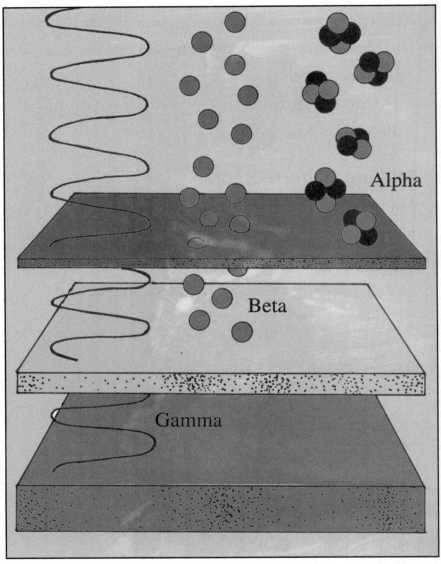

Alpha

Beta

Gamma

Scientists now know that lead will protect them from harmful radiation. Alpha particles can be blocked by paper and beta particles can blocked by brass, but only lead can block gamma rays

3. Tape the card to the straw. At room temperature, note the height of the water in the straw. Mark the height on the card.

4. Place the bottle in a sunny spot for one hour. Note the height of the water in the straw. Mark the height on the card.

5. Place the bottle in a shallow pan filled with ice water. Note the height of the water in the bottle. Mark the height on the card.

Measuring Heat Rays

The sun gives off heat rays. So does fire. Heat rays radiate outward in straight lines in all directions. In this experiment, you can measure heat rays.

Materials:

- a 100-watt light bulb
- a thermometer
- a piece of cardboard
- a pencil
- a sheet of paper

Procedure:

1. Switch the light bulb on. Leave it on for ten minutes.

2. Hold the thermometer four inches from the side of the bulb. Wait one minute. Write down the temperature.

3. Hold the thermometer four inches below the bulb. Wait one minute. Write down the temperature.

4. Hold the thermometer four inches from the side of the bulb. Place a piece of cardboard between the bulb and the thermometer. Wait one minute. Write down the temperature. It is lower because the rays will not pass through cardboard.

Observing the Decay of Molecules

You cannot handle radioactive materials, but in this experiment you can see one kind of decay process.

Materials:
- a small amount of luminescent, "glow-in-the-dark" paint (available at artists' supply stores)
- a 3' x 5' card
- a small paint brush

Procedure:

1. Brush some of the paint onto the card.

2. Hold the card in a bright light for one minute.

3. Take the card into a dark room. The paint will glow. Then the glow will slowly begin to fade.

The paint glows because light causes the paint molecules to become energized or "excited."

The glow fades and disappears because the molecules are losing their energy. They are decaying back to their "unexcited" or stable state. This process is very similar to the decay process in radioactive atoms.

There is an important difference between the paint molecules and radioactive atoms. When radioactive atoms decay, they change to non-radioactive atoms. The decay process ends when all the radioactive atoms are gone. In contrast, the paint molecules are not destroyed as they decay. They can be restored by again exposing them to a bright light.

CHRONOLOGY

1867—Marie Sklodowska is born in Warsaw, Poland (Russian Empire), on November 7.

1876—Sister, Zosia, dies.

1878—Mother dies.

1883—Graduates school.

1886—Marie becomes a governess.

1889—Moves back with her father.

1891—Enrolls at the Sorbonne.

1893—Earns her degree in physics.

1894—Earns her degree in mathematics.

1895—Marries Pierre Curie on July 26.

1897—Gives birth to her first child, Irene.

1898—Discovers two new elements, polonium and radium.

1903—Receives Ph.D. in physics on June 25.
Marie and Pierre receive the Nobel Prize for Physics jointly with Antoine Henri Becquerel for their work in the field of radioactivity.

1904—Gives birth to second daughter, Eve.

1906—Pierre is killed by a horse-drawn wagon on April 19.
Marie takes over Pierre's professorship and becomes the first woman to teach at the Sorbonne.

1911—Awarded a second Nobel Prize, this time for her work in chemistry.

1912—Becomes seriously ill but recovers.

1914—Paris Radium Institute opens with Marie as director. World War I begins.

1918—World War I ends.

Poland becomes an independent nation.

1921—Marie visits the United States and is presented with a gram of radium by President Warren G. Harding.

1926—Irene Curie marries Frederic Joliot.

1934—Marie Curie dies of leukemia, caused by exposure to radiation, on July 4.

1935—Marie's daughter, Irene Joliot-Curie, and her husband, Frederic Joliot-Curie, are awarded the Nobel Prize in Chemistry for their discovery of artificial radioactivity.

PERIODIC TABLE OF THE ELEMENTS

Periodic Table of the Elements

Group →	1	2	3	4	5	6	7	8
↓ Period								
1	1 H Hydrogen 1.008							
2	3 Li Lithium 6.941	4 Be Beryllium 9.012						
3	11 Na Sodium 22.99	12 Mg Magnesium 24.305						
4	19 K Potassium 39.10	20 Ca Calcium 40.08	21 Sc Scandium 44.96	22 Ti Titanium 47.88	23 V Vanadium 50.94	24 Cr Chromium 52.00	25 Mn Manganese 54.94	26 Fe Iron 55.85
5	37 Rb Rubidium	38 Sr Strontium 87.62	39 Y Yttrium 88.91	40 Zr Zirconium 91.22	41 Nb Niobium 92.91	42 Mo Molybdenum 95.94	43 Tc Technetium 98.91	44 Ru Ruthenium 101.1
6	55 Cs Cesium 132.9	56 Ba Barium 137.3	*	72 Hf Hafnium 178.5	73 Ta Tantalum 180.9	74 W Tungsten 183.8	75 Re Rhenium 186.2	76 Os Osmium 190.2
7	87 Fr Francium 223.0	88 Ra Radium 226.0	**	104 Rf Rutherfordium 261.1	105 Db Dubnium 262.1	106 Sg Seaborgium 263.1	107 Bh Bohrium 264.1	108 Hs Hassium 265.1

Key
6
C
Carbon
12.01

Atomic Number
Symbol
Atomic Weight

* Lanthanides	57 La Lanthanum 138.9	58 Ce Cerium 140.1	59 Pr Praseodymium 140.9	60 Nd Neodymium 144.2	61 Pm Promethium 146.9
**Actinides	89 Ac Actinium 227.0	90 Th Thorium 232.0	91 Pa Protactinium 231.0	92 U Uranium 238.0	93 Np Neptunium 237

Alkali metals	Alkaline earth metals	Lanthanides	Actinides	Transition
Poor metals	Metalloids	Nonmetals	Halogens	Noble g

State at standard temperature and pressure (0°C and 1 atm)			Natural occurrence		
Gases	Liquids	Solids	Undiscovered	Synthetic	From Decay	Prir

10	11	12	13	14	15	16	17	18
								2 He Helium 4.003
			5 B Boron 10.81	6 C Carbon 12.01	7 N Nitrogen 14.01	8 O Oxygen 16.00	9 F Fluorine 19.00	10 Ne Neon 20.18
			13 Al Aluminum 26.98	14 Si Silicon 28.09	15 P Phosphorous 30.97	16 S Sulfur 32.07	17 Cl Chlorine 35.45	18 Ar Argon 39.95
8	29 Cu Copper 63.55	30 Zn Zinc 65.39	31 Ga Gallium 69.72	32 Ge Germanium 72.61	33 As Arsenic 74.92	34 Se Selenium 78.96	35 Br Bromine 79.90	36 Kr Krypton 83.80
ium 4	47 Ag Silver 107.9	48 Cd Cadmium 112.4	49 In Indium 114.8	50 Sn Tin 118.7	51 Sb Antimony 121.8	52 Te Tellurium 127.6	53 I Iodine 126.9	54 Xe Xenon 131.3
um)	79 Au Gold 197.0	80 Hg Mercury 200.6	81 Tl Thallium 204.4	82 Pb Lead 207.2	83 Bi Bismuth 209.0	84 Po Polonium 209.0	85 At Astatine 210.0	86 Rn Radon 222.0
dtium .0	111 Rg Roentgenium 284.0	112 Uub Ununbium 288.0	113 Uut Ununtrium 293.0	114 Uuq Ununquadium 298.0	115 Uup Ununpentium 299.0	116 Uuh Ununhexium 302.0	117 Uus Ununseptium 310.0	118 Uuo Ununoctium 314.0

	64 Gd Gadolinium 157.3	65 Tb Terbium 158.9	66 Dy Dysprosium 162.5	67 Ho Holmium 164.9	68 Er Erbium 167.3	69 Tm Thulium 168.9	70 Yb Ytterbium 173.0	71 Lu Lutetium 175.0
ium 1	96 Cm Curium 247.1	97 Bk Berkelium 247.1	98 Cf Californium 251.1	99 Es Einsteinium 252.0	100 Fm Fermium 257.1	101 Md Mendelevium 258.1	102 No Nobelium 259.1	103 Lr Lawrencium 262.1

OTES:

s of 2006, elements 112–118 were still designated by the placeholder names sted.

s of 2006, element 117, ununseptium, had not yet been discovered. The atomic 'eight listed is a predicted number.

s of 2006, element 118, ununoctium, had not yet been discovered. The atomic 'eight listed is a predicted number.

CHAPTER NOTES

Chapter 1. Marie's Childhood Years

1. Eve Curie, *Madame Curie* (Garden City, N.Y.: Doubleday, Doran & Co., 1937), p. 211.

2. Ibid., p. 220.

3. Rosalynd Pflaum, *Grand Obsession* (New York: Doubleday, 1989), p. 5.

4. Curie, p. 51.

Chapter 2. A Broken Heart

1. Eve Curie, *Madame Curie* (Garden City, N.Y.: Doubleday, Doran & Co., 1937), p. 58.

2. Rosalynd Pflaum, *Grand Obsession* (New York: Doubleday, 1989), p. 18.

3. Curie, p. 80.

4. Susan Quinn, *Marie Curie* (New York, Simon and Schuster, 1995) p. 82.

Chapter 3. Freedom

1. Eve Curie, *Madame Curie* (Garden City, N.Y.: Doubleday, Doran & Co., 1937), p. 109.

2. Denis Brian, *The Curies* (John Wiley and Sons, Inc. 2005), p. 38.

3. Curie, p. 113.

4. Ibid., p. 129.

5. Ibid., p. 155.

Chapter 4. An Exciting Discovery

1. Eve Curie, *Madame Curie* (Garden City, N.Y.: Doubleday, Doran & Co., 1937), p. 157.

2. "Marie Curie—Research Breakthroughs (1897–1904)," *Marie Curie and the Science of Radioactivity*, 2006, <http://www.aip.org/history/curie/resbr2.htm> (June 13, 2006).

3. Curie, p. 168.

Chapter 5. Problems

1. Eve Curie, *Madame Curie* (Garden City, N.Y.: Doubleday, Doran & Co., 1937), p. 192.

2. Ibid., p. 191.

3. Rosalynd Pflaum, *Grand Obsession* (New York: Doubleday, 1989), p. 107.

4. Ibid., p. 103.

Chapter 6. A Tragedy

1. Eve Curie, *Madame Curie* (Garden City, N.Y.: Doubleday, Doran & Co., 1937), p. 211.

2. Ibid., p. 217.

3. Ibid., p. 222.

4. Ibid., p. 242.

5. Ibid., p. 246.

6. Ibid., p. 247.

7. Ibid., p. 252.

Chapter 7. Life Without Pierre

1. Eve Curie, *Madame Curie* (Garden City, N.Y.: Doubleday, Doran & Co., 1937), p. 254.

2. Ibid., p. 252.

3. Ibid., p. 284.

Chapter 8. A World at War

1. Eve Curie, *Madame Curie* (Garden City, N.Y.: Doubleday, Doran & Co., 1937), p. 287.

2. Ibid., p. 298.

3. Rosalynd Pflaum, *Grand Obsession* (New York: Doubleday, 1989), p. 201.

4. Curie, p. 305.

Chapter 9. A Trip to the United States

1. "Marie Curie—The Radium Institute (1919–1934)," *Marie Curie and the Science of Radioactivity*, 2006, <http://www.aip.org/history/curie/radinst1.htm> (June 13, 2006).

2. Eve Curie, *Madame Curie* (Garden City, N.Y.: Doubleday, Doran & Co., 1937), p. 324.

3. Ibid., p. 327.

4. Ibid., p. 347.

Chapter 10. An Ordinary Day

1.-"Marie Curie—The Radium Institute (1919–1934)," *Marie Curie and the Science of Radioactivity*, 2006, <http://www.aip.org/history/curie/radinst1.htm> (June 13, 2006).

2. Eve Curie, *Madame Curie* (Garden City, N.Y.: Doubleday, Doran & Co., 1937), p. 348.

3. Ibid., p. 366.

4. Ibid., p. 375.

Chapter 11. The End

1. Eve Curie, *Madame Curie* (Garden City, N.Y.: Doubleday, Doran & Co., 1937), p. 378.

2. Ibid., p. 381.

3. Ibid., p. 383.

GLOSSARY

active element—An element that gives off radiation.

atom—A tiny particle composed of a nucleus and electrons. Atoms make up the various elements.

conductor—A substance or body that can transmit electricity or heat.

element—A substance that is made of only one kind of atom.

intensity—The measurement of radiation's strength.

ionize—To cause to become a conductor.

molecule—A group of atoms that are bonded together.

pitchblende—An ore that contains uranium, polonium, and radium.

polonium—A radioactive element.

radiation—The process by which energy is given off by molecules and atoms.

radioactivity—The property of giving off rays of energy.

radiology—The study of radioactive substances.

radium—A radioactive element.

uranium—A radioactive element.

X-rays—Rays that can pass through various solid objects but not through bone.

FURTHER READING

Birch, Beverly. *Marie Curie: Courageous Pioneer in the Study of Radioactivity*. Woodbridge, Conn.: Blackbirch Press, 2000.

Cobb, Viki. *Marie Curie*. New York: DK Publishing, 2008

Krull, Kathleen. *Marie Curie*. New York: Viking, 2007.

McClafferty, Carla Killough. *Creating Something Out of Nothing: Marie Curie and Radium*. New York: Farrar Straus Giroux, 2005.

Pasachoff, Naomi. *Marie Curie and the Science of Radioactivity*. New York: Oxford University Press, 1997.

Steele, Philip. *Marie Curie*. New York: National Geographic Society, 2006.

Waxman, Laura Hamilton. *Marie Curie*. Minneapolis, Minn.: Lerner Publications, 2003.

Index